PUSHING THE GENERATIONS FORWARD

D1640714

PUSHING THE GENERATIONS FORWARD

FINDING YOUR PURPOSE THROUGH THE NEXT GENERATION

KWAMANE O. HARRIS, MBA, CPLC

XULON ELITE

Xulon Press Elite
2301 Lucien Way #415
Maitland, FL 32751
407.339.4217
www.xulonpress.com

EXULON
ELITE

Paperback ISBN-13: 978-1-66285-573-3
Ebook ISBN-13: 978-1-66285-574-0

Dedication

This book is dedicated to Annette A. Binns, the woman who persevered so that I could be revered. My mother, my best friend, and my spiritual coach.

Table of Contents

"Stop imitating the ideals and opinions of the culture around you, but be inwardly transformed by the Holy Spirit through a total reformation of how you think. This will empower you to discern God's will as you live a beautiful life, satisfying and perfect in his eyes."

Romans 12:2 TPT

SANKOFA

The concept of "Sankofa" is derived from King Adinkera of the Akan people of West Africa. "Sankofa" is expressed in the Akan language as Sankofa bird "se wo were fi na wosan kofa a yenki." Literally translated, this means "it is not taboo to go back and fetch what you forgot".

"Sankofa" teaches us that we must go back to our roots in order to move forward. That is, we should reach back and gather the best of what our past has to teach us, so that we can achieve our full potential as we move forward. Whatever we have lost, forgotten, forgone, or been stripped of can be reclaimed, revived, preserved, and perpetuated.

Visually and symbolically, "Sankofa" is expressed as a mythic bird that flies forward while looking backward with an egg (symbolizing the future) in its mouth.

*https://www.uis.edu/africanamericanstudies/students/sankofa/

Introduction

What I have learned in my life is that you cannot change a thing that has happened to you.

Looking back, I can admit that I would not change a thing. Yes, of course, I had to deal with the pain and anxiety of growing up in a single-parent household. No, I did not have the comfortable upbringing as a child that others have had. And yes, I still am working through some of the trauma and emotional scar tissue from the pain that I have experienced.

But looking at what I have learned, who I have become, and how I can impact others, I wouldn't want it any other way. Our minds try to make sense of everything we experience; it's how we learn and grow. That same analysis often comes with the side effect of making it impossible to move forward, to grow, and to forgive both ourselves and the circumstances that brought us to where we are.

It's perfectly normal for us to stop and dwell on the past, to look at it, and to remember a time when the troubles that we face now did not exist. It's when we start to require that past issues be fixed or changed that we cause our lives to be put on hold.

Our mind is essentially both our greatest friend and greatest enemy in this way. It's when we regain control of our mind—the control that we were always meant to have over our own thoughts, desires, and actions—that we then remember that all that ever happened to us was that we lost our way. Everything that is lost can be found again.

If you picked up this book, it is for you!

This book is for the person who has made a lot of mistakes. It is for the person who may be deciding to give up on life. It is for all of you who are lost and hurt that I've written this to show what our next step should be. It is for us, and, more importantly, the generations that will come after us.

My hope is that after you read this book, you will make a commitment to forgive yourself, forgive the people that have caused you hurt in life, and commit to the Pushing the Generations Forward movement.

The next generation will depend on you making that commitment. I have made a commitment in my personal life to do everything that I can in order to help the coming generations. I want my future children and grandchildren to have the necessary information and knowledge to create a life that is better than my own. The sacrifices that my mother, stepfather, grandmothers, grandfathers, and others in my life made has set me up to be who I am today. Because they worked so hard, I am now in a place where I do not have to worry about where my next meal will come from or whether I can afford college for my future children. I am blessed, and I can say without a doubt I understand my purpose.

However, I would be remiss to leave it there. It is my obligation to build upon what my mother and family did for me. It is the obligation of every generation to build upon what was built for them, and that is my message: push the generations forward.

Pushing the Generations Forward

To my educators, at-risk youth program staff, mentors, coaches, out-of-school-time staff, and anyone who directly or indirectly works with youth.

I wrote this book with all of you in mind. I have been in youth development and human services my entire professional career, and I know without a shadow of doubt that you all push the future generations forward. Every day you are met with unprecedented human challenges, and you somehow, someway, meet the needs of the young people. That's pushing the generations forward!

Often your work goes unnoticed and undervalued, but what you are doing matters. It not only matters to the current generation, but to the generations that will come behind them. Your work is instrumental in making the world a better place. Your sacrifices are more than we can ever fully know. You are a perfect example of pushing the generations forward. Thank you for all that you do.

My hope is that when you read this book, you will be able to understand that you are helping multiple generations by just helping one generation.

Chapter One

The Table Mindset

If you aren't at the table making decisions about your life, then where are you? You are probably on the agenda. Who do you want at the table making decisions about your life?

Growing up, I saw firsthand the importance of a strong mindset from my mother, who mentored me in how to thrive in a world that often keeps you from doing so.

I have always wondered what separates those of us who saw something that greatly developed our coping abilities and gave us the tools to deal with the many issues that our world throws at us. In this search, I've come to believe that, often, the greatest difference is maybe the most obvious one: some of us saw, and some of us didn't.

What this means is that some of us saw a great example living before us, and others did not have that example. Everyone's story is different, and each one prepared us in different ways for life. Some friends of mine seem to deal very well with sudden changes, like a sudden move, a new job, or maybe even something tragic like losing a loved one. Others seem to struggle when the same things happen. Each person has developed coping abilities to deal with different issues in life. Our own life experiences affect our lives in some way, and mine happened to encourage the development of a strong mindset.

Growth vs Fixed Mindset

The Pushing the Generations Forward movement requires a transformation of the mind, transcending the systems of thought you already have, and truly comprehending the concepts outlined in this book. Now, if you are willing to revel in the experience of reading this book, then you must first acknowledge that the idea in and of itself will not work if you are unable to adopt the mindset necessary to make it work. It is as good an idea as its execution allows for.

Before we can get into the topic of altering or evolving our mindsets, we must define what a "mindset" is. The definition we will use is this: A mindset refers to our perceptions and beliefs about what we can and cannot do. It also defines our qualities, such as our talents, creativity, and understanding of the world around us. When we adopt a growth mindset, we program our subconscious mind to believe that our skills, talents, and abilities can be developed or improved over time. (Carol S Dweck, 2007)

Given the effect that our mindset has on our life, the need to quietly consider these implications cannot be overstated. It takes time and effort to challenge a mindset that is fixed and to rise above that barrier. Approaching this task requires hard work and a serious commitment to critically analyzing our own mentality in order to bring about the conditions that can see the generations pushed forward.

It starts with a simple and remarkable premise: you must wholeheartedly believe, without a shadow of a doubt, that you can change anything about your life for the better. No matter what has happened, I believe with all my heart you can change it for the better. You cannot allow your past to dictate your mindset for the future.

This is not a shrugged off remark that you just smile at, think about occasionally and then move on as if you never heard it. It's a powerful and transforming way of thinking. When this seed takes root, and if you allow it to grow, then it will branch out and shape everything that you do. You are the architect of your own life. This single premise entails such empowering strength that having a solid grasp of this will completely overturn constructs and ideas that have been given to you from every angle of marketing, society, and negatively minded people. Start from here, make it your first step, and the rest is a matter of practice.

How The Mind Works

The first step in transforming your mind is to understand how it works. Developing an understanding of this wonderful tool that you use to make decisions can help you to understand why the methods we use to change our mindset are set up the way that they are.

Dr. Carol Dweck, a former Harvard professor, developed an interest in students' attitudes about failure. What she found was that some students rebounded from failure fairly well, whereas others were devastated by even the smallest amount of failure. It was through her work that the terms "fixed mindset" and "growth mindset" came to be.

Let's make sense of this phenomenon with an example. When an athlete believes he or she could become a better-performing athlete or beat their previous accolades, then they will put in extra time and effort to become that better athlete that they know they can be, ultimately resulting in higher achievement. This describes a growth mindset, and it is a concept that is backed by the latest in neuroscience. (Carol S Dweck, 2007)

As I am not a brain expert, I will try to explain this in the most accessible way possible.

Brain neurons are information messengers that connect various parts of the brain. They must make the proper connections so that certain functions, such as vision or hearing, can manifest. Neurons are cells within the nervous system that transmit information to other nerve cells, muscle cells, or gland cells.

Most neurons are composed of three main elements: a cell body, an axon, and dendrites. The cell body contains the nucleus and cytoplasm. The axon extends from the cell body and often gives rise to many smaller branches before ending at nerve terminals. Once axons reach their targets, they form connections with other cells at synapses (these look like gaps between neurons). At the synapse, the electrical signal of the sending axon is transmitted by chemical neurotransmitters to the receiving dendrites of another neuron, where they can either provoke or prevent the generation of a new signal. (BrainFacts/Sfn, 2012)

New advances in neuroscience have taught us that connectivity between neurons can change with experience. With enough practice, neural networks can grow new connections, strengthen existing ones, and build insulation that speeds the transmission of impulses (Mindset Works , n.d.)

Self-Belief

Scientific jargon aside, there are two main principles that will determine a successful outcome for those who desire self-improvement: self-belief and action.

Self-belief is the first step for anyone to take control of their mind. Using the same example as above, if an athlete believes he or she can give a superior performance with further practice and continues to repeat workouts and activities in pursuit of this goal, the neurons will grow new connections and strengthen older connections. This will, in turn, reinforce the belief that the athlete can do better and obtain a higher level of achievement. After all, if you can believe it, you can achieve it.

You have to believe in the impossible. You have to believe that each day is a new moment, a different opportunity, and you can never predict what each day will present you with. Making your belief in your potential strong will keep you observant and open to new possibilities as they come along. If you can cause your self-belief to snowball around past success, this cascade of positive reinforcement will keep you moving no matter the future obstacles you face.

This isn't achieved overnight, but it can be achieved nonetheless. Give yourself grace for past mistakes because you can't go forward with backward facing perspectives. There's a reason that we move on, and there's a reason that we face forward. We march to new possibilities every day. If our past dictated our present, and if each new moment was anchored by the one before it, then we would still be cavemen. It's our belief that drives us forward.

Positive Action

The second principle of developing a strong mindset is taking positive action. While the power of self-belief is undeniable, it is pretty worthless unless paired with subsequent action.

As you develop your mind and start to believe in your ability to better your life and the lives of those around you, you will need to start taking action. Standing still is the enemy of progress. While it's probably not so hard for you to picture what your goals are, to see them in front of you, and to almost know exactly what you want, it is, by contrast, much harder to develop the plans necessary to bring those dreams into reality.

There's no substitute for action, and there are no shortcuts. The process of developing a strong mindset is grounded in the ability of that mindset to drive positive action and the ability of that positive action to encourage self-belief to flourish even more. Taking the steps necessary to push generations forward involves taking positive steps toward everyday actions that will serve to constantly build you up. The process of taking positive action works in a similar fashion to the example of the athlete presented earlier in this chapter. When an athlete is training for something, they train daily, rest often, and ensure that they are putting themselves in optimal condition for success. For that athlete, success may look like running an extra mile, sleeping eight hours a night, ensuring they drink enough water, or making sure that they are studying the actions taken by another great athlete in order to be successful. Transfer this same principle to a more generic setting, and those actions can look like anything that moves you toward the goals that you have set for yourself.

Grit and Resilience

A guaranteed result of taking action and trying to better your life is the arrival of distractions and discouragements.

Isaac Newton's third law of motion states: "for every action, there is an equal and opposite reaction." In other words, when you do something good, there will be an equal and opposite force that tries to fight your actions. Each time you push off from where you are to try and accomplish something, there is a force pushing you back. This is why there is so much struggle behind breaking out of comfort zones and attempting anything that is difficult for you.

It takes time and effort to make anything happen. The push back at you can look like a lot of things, but the most common one to get people down and to prevent their growth are distractions.

The things that make us more likely to slow down and give up are rarely the most obvious. Distractions are everywhere, keeping you from looking straight ahead. Destructive self-hatred and negative self-talk are sometimes very present in your mind. No matter your story, you'll face resistance. But for some, the resistance is harder and more demoralizing.

Here is where we stop and determine to develop grit and resilience. Often used interchangeably, these two terms have behind them the meaning of taking the hits that life gives you but having the ability to come back after and to keep going on. When pursuing a stronger, newer mindset, you'll be facing obstacles along the way that seem insurmountable. But if you are going to make it and are going to be able to tackle the next issues around the corner, then you will need them to get you there.

Grit and resilience are what allows you to take the issues head on and to not let them keep you down. They'll wake you up in the morning after a rough night, and they'll keep your heart from feeling that it can't take anymore after you've fought for so long just to stay strong.

Developing these looks more like mentality than it does practice. You cannot just go around putting yourself in harm's way to develop resilience. When your thoughts come to you and you start to feel that there is no hope and that you simply won't ever beat the pressures holding you back, talk to yourself and learn how you react to these thoughts. Learn and know yourself better.

Generational Stability

Another concept of great importance is the principle of generational stability. The transition of a stable, well-lived life from generation to generation is a fundamental pursuit of people hoping to push the boundaries and to drive generations. It's one that those from broken homes long for and those from generational wealth and prosperity thrive on.

This is perhaps the more difficult concept to digest in depth. Let's say you are serving time inside a jail or penitentiary compound when reading this book—you feel like you have made some regrettable mistakes in life, and you want to start over and try again, but you feel like it's almost impossible given all the things you have endured or done in your past. Maybe you even feel hopeless because you think "the system" has been set up for you to fail.

If you decide to keep that mentality, every single day will have the same outcome: no progress. However, if you decide to look past all of that and take on the growth mindset, then you should also understand that any changes in your lifestyle are not just for you.

While it is tempting to think that the changes we make are for our own benefit only, the truth is that each of our actions has long-lasting ripple effects, and they benefit generations. It's for your children and your children's children. The changes that you experience and bring about can work toward generational stability. Your only promise to your children is that they will never have to endure the hardships you have had to endure in life.

What about the freshman athlete from what some may call "the ghetto"? He or she should understand that their high level of achievement is not for them solely; it's also for their enduring legacy. The successes and the failures of that individual go far past their time here on earth. Everything you do for the better in your life will be for the betterment of the generations that come after you.

The last concept is this: seek first to understand as opposed to being understood. As you take on the concept of Pushing the Generations Forward, most people won't understand your growth or even what it is you are trying to accomplish, and you should not expect them to. You will have some people that will doubt you and go against your new ideas, but understand that they are in a different place than you and they haven't allowed their mind to grow in the areas you have allowed your mind to grow. Their negativity and fears are a projection of their own inadequacies and insecurities.

That is why your actions are far more important than just saying what you believe; you must apply what you believe. Applying yourself this way is an example of a growth mindset.

Where are you today?

It's a question that I ask myself nearly every single day. While this might seem a bit strange, it is a question that holds great value to me.

Hopefully, after reading this book, or even just this chapter, you will begin to ask yourself the same question at least once or twice a week.

Let me provide you with some necessary backstory as to why this question is so important to me and why it's important in developing the table mindset.

About three years ago, I was attending my home church in Virginia. I don't remember the exact date, but I do remember it being the month of February because the church service was dedicated to Black history.

Upon entering, I thought it was going to be a typical Black history service, you know? Sing a few songs, hear a couple of speeches that are supposed to make you feel proud about being African American, eat soul food with everyone, and go home.

Most of the service went as planned, and it was not until the last speech that I realized this speech would be far from the usual I heard at other Black history programs. As the speaker was entering the room, I couldn't help but chuckle.

Walking in with an air of gravitas, he was donning an old slave outfit, and his hair, which was actually a wig, was puffy and gray. I muttered to myself, "Who does this guy think he is? Frederick Douglass?"

Well, as it turns out, that is exactly who he was playing that night.

I was acutely aware of how important Frederick Douglass was and what his legacy meant to African American history, so I was intrigued to hear what he might have to say.

You see, Frederick Douglass was no ordinary man in terms of slave rebellion, or what is known as abolitionism. We could easily talk about how, as a Black man, he served under five presidents, holding high appointed federal positions, or how as part of the Equal Rights Party ticket in 1872, Frederick Douglass was once selected as a candidate for vice president of the United States and as a running mate for the first female candidate, Victoria Woodhull. We could talk about how he taught a number of slaves to read and write, and how he wrote an open letter to his former slave owner in the North Star, the newspaper he created and published, criticizing his former slave owner on the evils of slavery and the enduring impact on his life.

But that is not what I want to focus on in this book; rather, I want to focus on one particular thing that Frederick Douglass did that I believe is probably the most profound and important thing any man could have done both in today's age and in the 1870s.

Now, to my surprise, the impersonator also thought this was important because he decided to deliver this speech to us during the Black history service. It was the speech that Frederick Douglass delivered on July 5, 1852, entitled "What to the Slave is the Fourth of July?"

The Frederick Douglass impersonator delivered his speech with a passion and fury I hadn't seen in a while, and it was contagious. It was as if we were the crowd that invited a former slave to celebrate America's freedom and independence.

He recounted the words that Douglass most likely used to prove his argument even further: "Do you mean, citizens, to mock me, by asking me to speak to-day?" Frederick Douglass thought it was a slap in the face to ask a former slave to speak on America's freedom and independence when African Americans across the country were still being held captive and in bondage to their white slave owners:

"What, to the American slave, is your 4th of July? I answer: a day that reveals to him more than all other days in the year, the gross injustice and cruelty to which he is the constant victim. To him, your celebration is a sham."

I was truly mesmerized by the presentation and cadence of the Frederick Douglass impersonator and how he played his role to the exact thought that I had about Douglass himself. The Douglass impersonator conveyed some truly powerful ideas and left me speechless by his presentation.

During the closing of his speech, he asked the very question that I asked you at the beginning of this section: "Where are you today?"

When he first asked the question, I'll admit, I was a little puzzled— probably like you were when I asked it previously.

He gave the crowd a stare, knowing that no one would really answer the question aloud, before explaining how we should answer the question. He said, "Where are you today? Are you at the table, or are you on the agenda?"

He went on a little further to say, "Are you doing everything you can to ensure that you are at the table making decisions about your life, or are you allowing someone else to sit at the table for you, making decisions about your life?"

It was at this moment that I was blown away by these words. That's when it hit me. That's when I found the words for the purpose of my life.

This was right around the time when college was really difficult for me, and be assured that I was not academically challenged, but rather, financially. I struggled to justify staying in college, simply because I could not afford it. While you may hear sacrificial stories of people working themselves to the bone to get themselves through college, I simply had no desire to follow in their footsteps. To me, the idea that I would spend all my precious time—the one resource you cannot get back in life—at work felt criminal. I had been there, done that, and I hated working two or three jobs just to save up enough money to pay for college each semester, so my refusal here was not ill-informed. Since I was the first person in our family to ever attend college and to later on graduate, my parents and family were supportive of me and did everything they could to help, but resources were limited.

I was ready to give up; I didn't see the purpose of this struggle. The cliché statement of going three steps forward and getting knocked two steps back was never truer than at this moment in my life. I was ready and resolute in my decision to quit college until hearing the Frederick Douglass impersonator speech that night, which changed my mindset completely to a growth mindset.

I call my mentality at the time the "Table Mindset." That night gave me new motivation and enabled me to find a purpose for my life. I came to the rightful conclusion that everything I do and have done will be to obtain and maintain my own seat at the table, and I will never be on the agenda, allowing someone else to make decisions about my life. If I wanted that seat, I had to work for it. That would be my work from that day on.

I want to be the one at the table making decisions about my life because, for far too long, people who don't understand what I have been through as a Black man and minority in this country have been making decisions about me without ever walking a single step in my shoes.

Now, this mindset doesn't just pertain to me as an individual, but it pertains to the people of my race: African Americans who have been marginalized and oppressed for many generations. The table has not been where we have been welcomed. And it's those years not being allowed there that have caused the plans and the ideas to be drawn up without our input and without us in mind.

Historically, the slave trade was a method of keeping African Americans away from life's proverbial table. Why do you think slave owners did not want slaves to learn how to read and write?

The answer is simple: knowledge is power. Frederick Douglass understood that it was important to be literate, and this is why he traded bread to the white children for lessons on how to read. If Frederick Douglass had not learned literacy, he would never have had the chance to advise presidents and hold high positions within the government during the height of slavery. Denying slaves the right to an education was a strategic power move, which served to keep them useful only for hard labor.

With access to education, who knows what would have become of the people taken as slaves? We know nothing of their intellect, ambition, or aptitude. That was their way to the table.

Restraining that access to the table withholding a chair—that act held a power that would shape the lives of Black Americans for generations. During his time enslaved, Frederick Douglass risked his life for the pursuit of literacy and knowledge because he knew he was on the agenda and denied access to the table. So, he made his own way and pushed up to the table without an invitation. He took what was rightfully his and began to speak into the agendas without being asked. He took it because it belonged to him, just the same as it belongs to you and me. I believe Douglass conducted himself with the table mindset, and by doing so, he pushed the generations forward.

He pushed the generations forward for people like me to be able to go to college, to get an education, and even to write this book. If you are an African American reading this book, I want you to think about where you would be if Frederick Douglass, Martin Luther King Jr., Harriet Tubman, Malcolm X, or any prominent activist had not done what they had done for Black folks in America. The many ways these men and women pushed generations range from laws to education. It is through their examples that we have heroes and visionaries for when tomorrow's struggles face us.

They were also prime examples I talked about earlier. They knew that their action would not directly benefit them right away; they knew that it would benefit men like you and me today.

Dr. King, famous for stating that he "had a dream," has been the face of that notion of preparing the future for those to come.

Harriet Tubman, who could've made the safe and easy choice to stay behind and not face torture and possible death at the hands of her oppressors, made instead the hard choice to run to the North. Once she was safe there, she then made the choice to go back and to face even more danger that she didn't have to. Her life could've been a virtual luxury compared to the one that she had been born into. Instead, she took her place among the many movers by leaving that comfort and running back through danger yet again. She did this several times, eventually even leading troops to go liberate her people. She lost so much that she was not required to lose. And she did it so that others after her would never be faced with the same choices that she had to face.

And, finally, a story of pushing the generations would not be complete without the words of Malcolm X: "Education is the passport to the future, for tomorrow belongs to those who prepare for it today." Knowing completely that he was responsible for the education of the future generations, Malcolm X faced death threats. His home was set on fire, his family suffered, and he was murdered—all because he was willing to push generations forward. He paid the ultimate price and suffered for it so that others could live. That's Pushing the Generations Forward in its highest form.

So, I ask you again: Where are you today? Are you at the table, or are you on the agenda?

If you have to second guess where you are, then chances are you are on the agenda. If there is uncertainty, then it is likely that you are not in the planning, that you are watching the powers that be transform you and shape you into something that you don't want to be. You know you are the architect of your own life, but you've given someone else the plans to edit how they see fit.

To the men and women sitting behind bars, and to the youth that spend most of their time fooling around in class because they were not taught the importance of being at the table: Where are you today?

Where have you been most of your lives? At the table? Or on the agenda?

To the people who have to resort to selling drugs: where are you today? To the person that has been battling with drug addiction for most of their life: where are you today?

To the person that wants to quit and give up: If you quit, where will you be? At the table? Or on the agenda?

If you can take on the burdens that those who went before you faced, then you will shift from being planned to planning. If you take on the mindset required to push the generations forward, then you will realize that you must do everything in your power to be at the table and then—and only then—we can begin to push the generations forward.

"I may not live to see our glory, but I will gladly join the fight, and when our children tell our story, they'll tell the story of tonight. Raise a glass to freedom, something that they can never take away, no matter what they tell you. Raise the glass to the four of us. Tomorrow there will be more of us, telling the story of tonight." – Hamilton, Lin Manuel Miranda

Chapter Two

Sankofa

"It is not taboo to fetch what is at risk of being left behind."

Now, you might be surprised to learn that the concept of pushing forward the coming generations is backed up by African tradition. I certainly was. The concept of Pushing the Generations Forward is not a new concept; it's just a new phrase to coin the term, but the idea is rooted in centuries of African culture. In fact, the concept has another term in West Africa: Sankofa.

"Sankofa" is an African word originating from the Akan tribe in Ghana. The literal translation of the word and the symbol is "it is not taboo to fetch what is at risk of being left behind." The word breaks down into three meanings: "San" (return); "Ko" (go); and "Fa" (look, seek and take). The Akan people believed in the importance of knowledge and the quest for information from the past in relation to the preservation of the future.

The Akan people even have a symbol for the term Sankofa; most people call it the Sankofa Bird. You will find that same symbol in this book. The mythical bird has its feet planted forward, his head looking backward, and is carrying its offspring on the journey to enlightenment, progression, knowledge, and optimism. The Akan people believe that there must be movement and new learnings, but we are also supposed to take what we have learned from the past to preserve its knowledge and wisdom and therefore make a better future.

Learn from the Past; Don't Live in It

Our past is our past for reason. For most people, when you think of the past, you either recall the bad memories or the nostalgic good ones. I believe that is exactly why the concept of Sankofa is so important.

Many people today are living emotionally in the past. They still feel the pain and the hardship that they did when they first experienced the trauma that shaped how they think today. If you are reading this book, you have probably made some mistakes in life—we all have. It might be the defining trait of being human. The level of mistakes varies between readers, but you may have made some mistakes that have cost you a great deal of something.

Because of the trauma and pain associated with many mistakes, we hold on to them in a negative way. Our mistakes cause us to avoid similar situations and to create walls and barriers. As humans, we should always look to learn from our mistakes. Our mistakes make us who we are, and while mistakes do not define you, what you learn from them does.

This concept becomes even harder when we are addressing the mistakes of others. We may burn ourselves on the hot stove and thus learn not to touch the hot stove, but what if someone burns us? Are we as quick and able to learn the lesson? Or do we simply focus on the pain we experienced?

The concept of Pushing the Generations Forward allows you to shift your mindset past the mistakes themselves and on to their teachable moments. No one is perfect at making this shift to calling their mistakes "teachable moments." However, this is exactly how we need to view the past. Sankofa embodies that concept: being able to preserve and move forward no matter what happened in the past, and using the past for learnings to pass on to the future generations.

"Don't Count Your Chickens Early"

I am from the South, and if the old folks from the South are known for anything, it's their rich traditions and great wisdom. Growing up, I found myself always wondering how the older folks gained so much wisdom. Why did they tell young people to refrain from certain lifestyle choices? Why did they always have a lesson regarding some of the life choices that you were about to make?

I recall one powerful lesson that my grandmother taught me. I was just starting my lawn service business at the age of eleven—and by lawn service business, what I am referring to here is me just going out and cutting my neighbors' grass every two weeks and going door to door to find new clients.

After weeks and weeks of trying, I finally built a pretty good size clientele. I can remember waking up one Saturday morning and mowing the lawns of five of my neighbors for fifteen dollars each. That is seventy-five dollars, and at eleven years old, I had never made that much money in my short lifetime.

I was so proud of myself that I ran home and showed my grand-mother and immediately started telling her what I was going to do with my money. I cannot remember what I wanted to buy exactly, but I know that the amount of money that I needed to save in order to buy it was quite a lot. So, I started going over a plan to make sure I cut those yards every two weeks and began counting money I hadn't made yet.

When she saw my excitement, she stopped me and said, "That's good, Grandson, but don't count your chickens before they hatch."

That was a teachable moment that I have never forgotten to this day. What she was saying was obvious: "I know you have a plan for how you are wanting to achieve the money goal, and I know that you are looking forward to achieving the money goal, but you cannot account for the unseen variables that may come into effect when trying to achieve your goal."

I have tried to take this with me, but I think it's still so easy to do. How often do we make plans, hope to see them come true, and get excited, only to be disappointed when they don't work out and we are left feeling empty? I learned from her that day, and as time went on and I continued to make decisions in my life, I realized how right she actually was.

I found out later in life that it was a mistake she made in her younger days that she had to learn from that instilled in her this wisdom. She turned her mistake into a teachable moment and passed on that knowledge to me. Right then, my grandmother pushed the generations forward by teaching me something that resonated with me my entire life, and ever since that day, I have tried my best to not "count my chickens before they hatch."

I know it doesn't seem like much, but she pushed it forward. She allowed me to learn not just from my past, but from hers as well. There are many people in your life that have taught you something from their own experience. You didn't realize it, but they were setting you (the next generation) up for a better life, free of the mistakes they once made. This wasn't my past I was learning from, but it was the past nonetheless.

In generational learning, this is how information is passed on. It's given as a warning to prevent the next generation from making the same mistakes as the last.

Passing it to The Next Generation

When most people think of Pushing the Generations Forward, they think it is all about money or doing something huge. But the truth is, pushing a generation forward can start with something simple, such as passing on wisdom and knowledge. The mistakes of the last generation, the lessons learned, the mindset achieved—all of these things are assets that the next generation can grow and benefit from.

Unfortunately, this passing-on process goes both ways. When there is a generational curse, this same principle applies. The damage, the pain, the harm—it all goes forward from generation to generation. The next several generations may have to be the ones to work harder if the last few didn't pull their weight.

Just as no man is an island and no one person is a lone wolf, no one generation is a static unaffected or unaffecting entity. They exist back-to-back, one affecting the next, and sometimes in reverse. Newer generations can help the still-living members of the older generation to make decisions later in life that help them grow.

What's important to remember is that the generations coming after you will always make their own choices; this is very true and irrefutable. There's no way to ensure their success with only material gains, although those do help significantly.

What is equally, if not more, important are the lessons taught to the next generation. Maybe you don't have the means to leave them with a trust fund or a large house. Maybe you aren't able to ensure they get an amazing education or live in a good part of town. You haven't failed if your contribution to their lives is simply the lessons that you have taught them. Lessons last longer than money and a home. Lessons last longer than the benefits of an education too. Memories, lessons, and precious pieces of advice make the greatest inheritance.

What is At Risk of Being Left Behind?

Are you leaving behind your peace, your joy, your integrity, or maybe your dignity? Are you leaving your true self behind because of the mistakes you made? Are you leaving your true self behind because of your past traumas? Are you leaving your true self behind because of who hurt you or who wasn't there? Those past traumas or mistakes are teachable moments, and it's not just okay, but it's also necessary, to learn from them.

When you look at the principle of Sankofa, it is important to bring back only what is important. It is easy to carry the trauma and make that our guiding light, but that shouldn't be the case. We need to "sift" through the memoires and find the lesson.

For example, my grandmother could've seen me trying to start a business and discouraged me because of her bad experience. She could've rationalized that it would save me the headache and pain of losing money if she just told me to stop and get a regular job or something like that.

But she didn't.

That's because she saw what was truly at risk of being left behind. She saw that if she could teach me an important money lesson at a young age, she could help me move forward in my finances for the rest of my life. What was at risk? My financial freedom. Other memories may have lessons that lead to spiritual, physical, or emotional freedom. As we look at our past memories, we have to look at it this way: find the lesson and leave the rest in the past.

Chapter Three

No Boots

"It's all right to tell a man to lift himself by his own bootstraps, but it is cruel jest to say to a bootless man that he ought to lift himself by his own bootstraps." - Martin Luther King Jr.

While you're on your journey of learning how to push the generations forward, you're likely to come into contact with this idea of someone pulling themselves up by their own bootstraps. If you take a look at the interview where this famous quote came from, Dr. King explicitly lays out the difference between a person with boots and a person without boots.

The difference between the man with boots and the man without them is one of actually being able to facilitate their own deliverance. This interview gives the listener, as it did back when it was originally aired, a way to see how the idea of deliverance is not as easy as one may like to believe that it is. The many people who live and work may have trouble lifting themselves up when they have nothing with which to lift themselves.

In 1967, at the Ebenezer Baptist Church in Atlanta, Georgia, Dr. King spoke with NBC News Reporter Sanders Vanocur. Sanders wanted to speak about "New Phase" and "Genuine Equality in America." (King, 1967)

I must admit, if I had seen this interview as a young bright-eyed child, I probably would not have truly understood what to make of it. The level of economic and racial injustice broken down in this interview by Dr. King would have gone above and beyond my level of thinking at such a young age, but, as the old folks used to say, "just keep on living."

Growing up in a society where the color of your skin is made a stigma constitutes a whole new level of self-deprivation. In fact, Dr. King talks about it in the NBC interview: "We all (negroes) have to deal with this feeling of constant nobody-ness."

I want you to think about living your entire life being constantly reminded that you are a nobody, and that you don't matter to the world around you. I am sure that everyone can relate to this very feeling. You don't have to be a certain color to feel this type of way, but it is particularly pervasive to people of color. I could really write another book about what that constant reminder does to a person, especially to minorities in the United States, but I want to focus on something else Dr. King stated in the interview: "It's all right to tell a man to lift himself by his own bootstraps, but it is cruel jest to say to a bootless man that he ought to lift himself by his own bootstraps."

Now before we get into that quote, which forms the basis upon which I write this chapter, I want to give you a little bit of backstory to the quote so that you might understand the impact of what Dr. King said.

Do You Have Any Idea?

I was intrigued by one of the questions that led up to the famous bootstraps quote by Dr. King. Sanders asked him, "Do you have any idea of what the negro wants to be in America?"

This question stunned me for a second, simply because I wondered how that was even a question. Of course, Dr. King knew! He was one of the greatest minds and advocates for civil rights and equality for African Americans!

And, before I knew it, I shouted the answer before Dr. King could answer in the video: "Black folks want to be treated like everyone else in America!"

Black people wanted to be given the same economic starting point as their white counterparts. Why would anyone think this answer would be different than any other race in America?

Sanders then asks, "What is it about the negro, every other ethnic group somehow, not easily … got around it? Is it just the fact that negros are Black?" Sanders was asking this question in regard to making excuses as to why the Black community could not rise up and make a better life for themselves.

This was where the famous Dr. King bootstrap quote was inspired from, but Dr. King also said something that I think answered both of Sanders's questions in the most intelligent way: "You cannot 'thing-a-fy' anything without depersonalizing that something. If you use something as a means to an end, at that moment, you make it a thing and you depersonalize it."

When the question "Do you have any idea of what the negro wants to be in America?" was asked, I believe the question itself reflected the very reason for the above response Dr. King gave. Africans were unwillingly brought to the Americas solely for the reason of free labor. That was the "thing-a-fication" of the Black race in America, and, as a result of that, slaves created the wealthiest country in the world as we know it today.

Most people know that slaves were not considered people or human beings by law at the time. Slaves were considered property. Slaves were used to pay off debt. Depending on the number of slaves in your possession, you were able to get a loan from the bank, and slave owners had to pay a sales tax on the slave when they were being sold.

This is, by its nature, dehumanization. No matter who you are, I encourage you to do some research on the real history of America during slavery, the Jim Crow era, and the civil rights movement. No matter who you are or where you're from, it is true that any rational human being would display a variety of emotions. I know when I first read the real facts about these terrible times in America's history, and not what they teach you in history books, I became deeply upset, and I felt less valued; I felt as if I was a nobody because of the color of my skin. In the same interview, Dr. King called it a constant sense of nobody-ness; it was "a sense of standing anonymous before the bar of history. Of having come from nowhere into a life bound for nothing."

Again, let me reiterate that you don't have to be a certain color to experience a constant sense of "nobody-ness," but here is where the concept of Pushing the Generations Forward forces out that mentality and feeling.

The Sad Reality

Most of us weren't given boots. The sad reality is that, while each generation needs to start off with at least feet to stand on, the many people that Dr. King was referring to then still have trouble gaining any boots now. No savings bonds, no land, no college savings, no trust fund, no rich parents, no three-story house that you can one day flip and sell for three times the price your grandparents bought it for. And so, they don't have a strong economic base to build their generational stability on.

And with this necessary context in mind, you often feel the urge to quit because it hurts too much to climb the thorny ladder of success without the necessary boots. And when most people quit, they don't just quit; they quit for something else.

Quitting of your own will is quite different from simply finding a replacement. So many times, things find their way into the inventory of those people who have had to give up everything in despair.

Speaking from the experience of a Person of Color (POC), it is far easier becoming an alcoholic than becoming a top-level executive for a major corporation. It's far easier settling for the high euphoric experience of crack, heroin, and cocaine than to become a cardiologist. It's far easier to sling drugs as a dealer than to become a chief product officer for Amazon or Google.

This sounds grim, but I can imagine you get the point. If you have ever been beaten down and boggled by society, then you understand the will to quit—especially for the people in America that have been constantly disenfranchised, disadvantaged, and disparaged—when you are constantly overlooked and overwhelmed.

Oppression is Real

Oppression is real, and one of the symptoms of oppression is the constant feeling of nobody-ness. I want you to think about oppression like most folks would think of a bully—the bully that constantly picks on you for years and years and tells you that you aren't worth anything, tells you that you won't ever amount to anything, and who supplies constant physical and emotional abuse that is burned into your mind and lasts even beyond the bullying.

You and I both know the severity of the consequences of the bully's actions. If the bully gets in your head long enough, you actually start to believe those negative things about yourself, and so, you become a depressed defeatist, you feel isolated, you feel hopeless, you feel like no one cares about you, that you don't belong in this world, and that your life doesn't matter. That is what oppression does to the human spirit.

I would like you to think about the oppression that you have faced in your life, and if in the unlikely circumstance that you have never faced oppression, then I want you to take your best guess at this and then I want you to consider what oppression could have done to your success ladder.

Hear me clearly: Just because you have felt that level of constant nobody-ness doesn't mean you can't overcome it. Just because you have been oppressed in the past doesn't mean you can't overcome it. Just because you weren't given boots with straps you could pull up doesn't mean you can't overcome it. In fact, that should be your motivation—that you alone can overcome anything.

I know you weren't given a good hand in life, but you have to play the cards you have been dealt. You may, in fact, know that those cards couldn't win a game even if your life depended on it.

However, who's to say you won't be dealt a new hand at some point? Who's to say that you cannot reach into the deck of cards and pull out the cards that you want to play with it? It's your deck of cards (life), and you make the rules. So, why not play a new game?

Finding Your Boots

When pushing generations forward, you have to let go of what has been done to you by society. You can't keep focusing on the negative situations and circumstances; rather, you need to focus your actions on ensuring that your children and their children will never experience and endure what you did in your lifetime.

Yes, oppression is real. Yes, the journey to success can be hard. Yes, you may not build the perfect world in your lifetime. That's why you can't give up. If you do, you make it harder for the people who are supposed to come after you.

Can you imagine if Dr. King would have given up? What if he said the dream for equality and justice for Black folks in America would be far too hard and walked away? What if Malcom X decided that the price that would have to be paid for equality in America was far too heavy and he decided that he didn't want to pay it? Where would America be right now?

This is the point I am trying to make. Giving up is not an option; in fact, not living to your fullest potential is no longer an option, either—it's imperative in today's society because of inflation, the job market, and generations depending on you. If you quit now, who knows what might happen to them? The boots that you need, the resources that you need, their scarcity, and there not being things that you were passed down to begin with are factors that can cause the best of us to give up. But we cannot afford to do that.

Giving Others Their Boots

The worst thing that we can do is make excuses. Yes, historically, African Americans have been treated as second-rate or worse. Yes, inflation is affecting our money. Yes, there are companies and politicians that still try to segregate and discriminate. But the reality is that in today's world, we have the opportunity to change that. My mom didn't have the ability to do what I do. She worked so that I could find myself in a better place.

The same is true for all of us. Our ancestors didn't have the ability to buy land or own a house. They were denied that right. But we can. We just have to make a decision to do it. That is the first step to finding your boots.

The second step is to find the route that you will take to get there. In today's world, we idolize financial freedom as the way to move our family forward. And I get it: a lot of freedom comes with not having to worry about money. However, there are other ways to find your boots.

Education is very important. Only when you are educated are you able to think for yourself and find the best way to overcome the hardships of life. Although it is universally recognized as important, education rarely is a lucrative job. However, it is very important to helping others to find their way.

Another way you can move the generations forward is through entertainment. The inspirational ability of music, movies, and other forms of entertainment is invaluable in helping others. How many times has a song or a scene from a movie helped you to get through a hard time? That is powerful.

Whichever route you choose, you must be ready to dedicate your life to it. Work like the future of the world depends on you—because it does.

Chapter Four

The Good Book and Spirituality

"Now Joseph and all his brothers and all that generation died, but the Israelites were exceedingly fruitful; they multiplied greatly, increased in numbers and became so numerous that the land was filled with them."

My faith is very important to me. Throughout my life, I have had my doubts, my ups and downs, and, at times, I was ready to give up. However, my faith would carry me through. A timely word, a friendly reminder, or even a strong correction helped me to get to where I am today.

This is not a religious self-help book or a devotional, but I would be remiss if I did not address the importance of embracing the spiritual nature of our being. To neglect our spiritual being would be to neglect a universal belief system. A belief system is critical for all human beings, and it's something that we all hold close and dear to our hearts by design. We cannot navigate this life without a blueprint of beliefs to follow, whether we are religious or not.

As a man of faith, I believe that Pushing the Generations Forward cannot happen without the understanding and the application of Jesus Christ. I know that many others have different beliefs, and I want to respect that.

But, I also want to challenge you. Study, seek, and search your belief system. Ask yourself why you believe what you believe. I believe if you are honest and if you are sincere, you will find Jesus.

While this chapter will make the most sense if you have a relationship with Him, the principles I teach can extend to anyone with a belief in God. My hope is that we can find the common ground and understand the principles that I believe are a crucial part of Pushing the Generations Forward.

Finding Your Purpose

In order to take on the task of pushing the generations forward, you must have a clear understanding of what you were created to do. Do you know what your purpose is? Do you know the specific thing that you were put on this world to do? The truth is that until you find your God-given purpose, you will always have a nagging sense of "nobody-ness" or emptiness. While everyone's life is going to be a bit different, our purpose is clear.

Throughout the Bible, God gives us reminders to love God and to love people. Probably the most popular connotation of this principle is the golden rule. While Jesus was teaching people how to live, a person asked him a question: "What is the greatest commandment?"

Jesus's answer was simple: "Love God with everything you have, and to love your neighbor as yourself." (Biblica, 1984)

Whether you agree with my Christian faith or not, we can agree that this should be the purpose of everyone on earth. If we started living our life to honor a moral power that is higher than ourselves and to treat those around us with respect and honor, we would answer most of the world's issues very quickly.

One thing that people confuse is "calling" and "purpose." Everyone has the same purpose, but our calling may be different. Let me explain.

Imagine a president of a company. He has dedicated much of his life to building a business and is considered by many to be extremely successful and important—and deservedly so. As a youth, he grew up in a moderate home—neither rich nor poor. He worked his way through college and climbed the corporate ladder. His name is on billboards and the lips of everyone around the country. He is, in many ways, quite famous.

More importantly, he is extremely devoted to his faith. Anyone who knows him knows he has a gentle heart, and his faith is an example to many. He gives to many organizations, spends a great deal of his personal time helping in his community, and does it all without cameras or press recordings. When asked about his faith and his charitable work, he shares: "Growing up, I made a promise: I would spend my life following God. My purpose is not money; it is to point others to God." Through his giving and his public platform, he is able to help thousands and inspire others to do the same.

Now, imagine a second individual. His story is not so grandiose. He works his entire life as a janitor at a local high school. He never makes more money than he can save. His family is fed, clothed, and taken care of, but they never have more than they need. He is a quiet man, but he is very dedicated to his faith. He volunteers as the janitor at his church, and everyone knows him as a faithful, quiet, and modest man. When he is not working, he makes sure to spend time raising his only son. His wife passed when they were younger, and he never remarried, but he committed to providing for his son. He never had money because he put it all away for his son to receive a college education.

What seems to be a glaring spot in his life's resume is that he turned down an offer to be president of a national janitorial company. This move would've transformed the life of him and his son, but he said no. When asked why, he answered, "When I was young, my wife and I prayed for a son. Before having my son, my wife and I promised God that we would raise him to follow Him. That job would've taken my time and kept me from keeping that promise."

Both of these men recognized they had a purpose. While their lives had different callings, one to be a janitor and the other to be a businessman, they both were able to move with conviction because they had a clear purpose: to point others to God. In order for you to take on this task of pushing the generations forward, you have to understand God's purpose for your life. If you do not have a basic understanding of your purpose, you will find yourself chasing all the wrong things.

We see this all the time in our culture. We chase women, cars, money, and status and eventually find out that none of that satisfies. This leads to an empty and, honestly, wasted life.

Imagine if you spent all the time reading, studying, and chasing one meaningful purpose in life, rather than chasing these material riches that we all inherently know will never provide fulfillment. I believe that finding our true purpose in life is the beginning of pushing the generations forward.

Spirituality – a Belief System

Again, no matter who or what you believe in, I posit that spirituality and loving God is critical to the human experience. I would go as far as arguing that the people who practice agnosticism (those who believe in the existence of God or a divine entity who is unknown or unknowable) or practice atheism (a view that one should live their life with no regard to a god or divine entity) are also practicing a form of spirituality. Spirituality has everything to do with your belief system, not organized religion. Whether you believe in an unknowing higher power or you don't believe in a higher power at all, you believe in your personal well-being, and those belief systems are clear for your purpose and happiness.

Spirituality is defined as the quality of being concerned with the human spirit or soul as opposed to material or physical things. The concept of spirituality directly relates to the reality that there is something greater than us, which we use as a divine guide to instruct us to a clear purpose. I could have started with any of the five aspects of personal health, but I choose spirituality first because I believe it's the most important; your belief system creates your values and purpose, and your values and purpose gauges your spiritual well-being. I would also argue that without a strong sense of spiritual well-being, you will not be able to maintain wellness in all the other four aspects of personal health.

"You cannot live well if you cannot get real." – Dr. Dharius Daniels, Pastor

As I stated earlier, in order to truly adopt the concept of Pushing the Generations Forward, you must understand your purpose. In the next chapter, I will talk about how I developed my purpose at eight years old, and how that purpose guided me well into and throughout my adult years. I knew that I wanted to be able to take care of my children's children, and so I allowed nothing to get in the way of me fulfilling that purpose. The questions you should stop and ask yourself are, "What is my purpose?" and "What am I meant to do here on this earth?"

If you are struggling to answer these questions, then I will follow up with these questions instead: What is your belief system?" By that, I mean, What are the principles by which you live your life, the ones that guide you? What values does your belief system create for you? And what does your belief system say about your purpose?

The reason why I stress purpose here is because purpose influences life decisions, impacts behaviors, and offers a sense of direction for your life, and I believe you can only find your sense of purpose once you fully understand your spiritual beliefs. What I love about the path of spiritual discovery is that you accidentally find yourself on the same path of self-discovery and, once you understand who you are, then I guarantee you will be able to understand your purpose in this life.

I will use my faith as an example. In the book of Jeremiah, the prophet Jeremiah predicted the falling of Judah, whose people were sent into exile by the Babylonians under the rule of King Nebuchadnezzar. After Jeremiah's prophecy came true and the people of Judah were sent into exile, Jeremiah sent letters to the surviving elders, priest, prophets, and all the people, telling them how long they were going to live in exile and what to do there. In exile, God still ensured that His people had purpose. In Jeremiah, chapter 29, verses 1-10, He gave them purpose by giving them direction and instructing them on what to do while in exile. God not only gave them purpose, but He gave them a sense of perspective: "For I know the plans I have for you, declares the Lord, plans to prosper you and not to harm you, plans to give you hope and a future" (Jer. 29-11).

It's an important aspect of my spirituality to understand that no matter where I am in life, whether in exile or in solitude, and no matter the mistakes I've made, God has a plan for my life. It has been written and destined. That plan is to prosper and to have hope for the future. That gives me some sense of purpose and the confidence necessary to achieve whatever I set out to do. My purpose gives me a reason to wake up in the morning and to be the best that I can be. I can always tell when I am living outside my purpose because I find it hard to get out of my bed in the morning and don't feel like I am living my best life.

Even after you find out what you are on this earth to do, you must also understand that your path to your purpose will not always be clear. Life happens, and sometimes life presents unanticipated events that make the path to your purpose unclear and certainly doubtful. Therefore, you must hold on to your purpose, even when the going gets tough.

In this life, you will constantly face what I call the psychological battleground. This mental battleground has everything to do with what you know to be true about yourself versus the perceived truth often inputted by other people, life events, mistakes, and shortfalls. The psychological battleground is very hard to navigate and instills you with doubts along the way; therefore, I stress the importance of spirituality.

On your spiritual journey, you will find purpose. Your purpose is your truth. If you are not spiritually mature enough to recognize truth over false perception, then you will lose the psychological battle. I know that God has a plan for my life, and that plan is to prosper and to have hope for the future, with the knowledge that anything outside that purpose is false perception.

> For though we live in the world, we do not wage war as the world does. / The weapons we fight with are not the weapons of the world. On the contrary, they have divine power to demolish strongholds. / We demolish arguments and every pretension that sets itself up against the knowledge of God, and we take captive every thought to make it obedient to Christ. (2 Corinthians 10:3-5)

In terms of my faith, Apostle Paul gives us direction by saying part of our purpose is to destroy strongholds. What are "strongholds"? They are mental blocks that do not allow you to see the full truth. A stronghold can be fear, guilt, resentment, insecurity, jealously, sense of failure, lack of confidence, anger, pride, etc. Believe your truth, win the arguments with yourself, and remember your purpose—live it, and build a solid foundation on the bedrock of spiritual wellness.

Relationship Over Religion

Often, people believe that there is a God, but they don't go to the next step. We view God as someone up in the sky that created us and, one day, will judge us. While this is true, this is also a very limited picture of who God is.

I like to think of the relationship of a child to their parent. In a sense, our parents are our creators. Usually, after we are born, our parents provide clothing, food, shelter—the necessities of life for the majority of our childhood. Along with that nourishment and care comes some basic rules or commandments. We are told to help with the house, brush our teeth, etcetera. All of this is an attempt to help us grow and mature as human beings.

Now, with exceptions, this care and commandment is not the end of the interaction with parents. In fact, this care and commandment leads to a desire for something more: a relationship. Eventually, we get to a point of sharing memories and thoughts with our parents, and we create an amazing relationship that can't be compared to anything else.

That is how we should be with God. He created us, and, yes, He gave us commandments to follow. While following His commandments is a great place to start, we should look to go beyond that; we should look to form a relationship. I believe this is something that many who practice religion—whether Christianity, Islam, or Hinduism—miss. They practice the religion but fail to build the relationship.

Finding Your Spirituality

However you were raised or whatever you believe, I encourage you to study and seek what you believe. Ultimately, our life will be changed when we find out where we came from, who we are, and consequently, what our purpose is in life.

Chapter five

My 8-Year-Old Self

This chapter starts with a question: What is your calling in life? What is the reason you exist on this earth? While our purpose can be dictated by our religious beliefs, we still have the duty and responsibility to understand our calling. While the two may sound similar, there is a slight difference.

Speaking from experience, finding your calling isn't as easy as some people might think it is. The journey to finding your purpose can feel like an impossible task, and what I know first-hand is it requires a great deal of patience and fortitude. It requires numerous taxing, emotional, physical, and mental sacrifices, as well as sleepless nights, leaving relationships with both family and friends, emotional hurt, physical pain, depression, anxiety—the laundry list of criteria goes on. The cost of finding your calling can feel like it's too expensive, and that's why some people quit while on that journey of finding their calling.

Now, as I stated in earlier in this book, when most people quit, they don't just quit; they often quit for something else. Meaning, they quit and allowed what they gave up on to be replaced by something that at least feels easier and may at first be less of a risk. It's easier to quit the path of finding your calling than to stay on that journey when you aren't quite sure where you will end up—especially if you know you will not like what you will discover when it's all said and done. If you want to fully embrace this concept of Pushing the Generations Forward, you must fully embrace that you must find your purpose.

We are all probably familiar with the famous quote, "The two most important days in your life are the day you are born, and the day you find out why" (Mark Twain). The path to finding your calling and the path of self-discovery are not mutually exclusive. You will find that once you find your calling in life, you will discover who you really are.

This, of course, includes the evergreen and introspective knowledge of why you think the way you do, why you behave the way you behave, why certain things bother you, and why you get so emotional about things others don't care about. Living without purpose is a very anxious life, and it is often led by undefined decisions and actions. That's a huge reason why finding your purpose is the first key to success and living the best life possible.

I believe we should think of purpose the same way most successful businesses think about goals for their companies or organizations. Goals typically represent an organization or company's larger purpose. If you think about any Fortune 500 company, they all have at least one thing in common: the ability to seek out a purpose or simply the ability to set goals. If Fortune 500 companies seek out their purpose to maximize shareholders' value, don't you think you should too?

The day you find out why, the day you find out your calling, should be your last day of being the old you. Make it the last day of your past life.

When you find out your purpose, you talk more eloquently, you carry yourself differently, you behave differently, and things that were once appealing to you are no longer appealing. People who bring no value or purpose to your life are no longer fun to be around. Discovering your calling doesn't just change you mentally; it changes you emotionally and socially. The places you thought you fit in don't really feel like a good fit anymore. The emotional passion you have toward your inner beliefs changes simply because you have a different way of thinking and feeling.

As we talked about earlier in the chapter, I remember the day I discovered my calling. I knew deep down inside that I had a strong calling in my life, but I could have never phrased it until that day at the Black history program. I've always felt that I was different and that something was calling me to be different. I knew that God had a calling on my life, but I just didn't know why—let alone, what that calling was. I could never quite put my finger on why I never really felt comfortable with the in-crowd, or why certain things just didn't appeal to me at an early age.

Then, one day, I remembered, and it just hit me all of a sudden. The reason why I didn't fit in or fall for temptation at an early age is because I made a promise to myself at eight years old. Until I was twelve years old, I grew up with a single mother of three, and, for years, I watched my mother work hard to take care of me, my brother, and sister. At that time, she didn't have a high school diploma, and yet, she still somehow managed to provide for us. My mother is the strongest woman I know and will forever be my hero.

My biological father, who, all throughout my childhood, battled with addiction and substance abuse, became a product of his environment. I remember everything we went through during those times of trial and tribulation. I remember watching my mother cry because she wanted to give up, but she couldn't—she had to keep going, or everything would fall apart without her. I remember her struggling to pay the rent just to keep a roof over our heads. I remember trips to the food bank just so that we could eat for the week. I remember boiling hot water just so that we could take a bath in the sink due to the water being cut off after my mother couldn't afford to pay the water bill. I remember walking through the house for weeks with no power. I remember it all, but I also remember the day I decided that when I grew up, I would give my mother what she deserved and make sure my mother and my family would never have to struggle again. I was about eight years old when I decided that. I knew at eight years old that I would make enough money to take care of all the worries my family was experiencing. I didn't know it yet, but at eight years old, I made a commitment to myself, which ultimately gave me purpose. That's probably the first time, without knowing it, that I wanted to push the generations forward.

I also knew at eight years old that I wanted to do it the right way; my biological father taught me early on what a life of addiction and incarceration could do for you: nothing good.

Football and Finding My Calling

My way out, as most young Black men think, was football. I knew I was an exceptional performer in sports, and I knew that if I worked hard, specifically on football, that I could use my natural talents and work ethic to make it to the league and be able to take care of my mother. I was so committed to that purpose that I often slept with a football by my side. It was my passion, not because I was good at it or because people praised me for it, but because I knew that I could take care of my family with it.

When I look at football, I see the perfect example of why you need to find your calling. When you are on a football team, everyone has the same purpose: to play football and win games. Every practice, every meal, every film watched, every tip and direction from your coaches is with that purpose in mind.

Now, imagine if that's where it stopped. Everyone is working hard to throw the ball, catch the ball, learn every play, and beat the other team, but something is missing. Did you catch it yet? Yes! What position does everyone play?

The best teams not only understand their purpose collectively as a team, but they also understand their individual calling or position. It does no good for a football team if everyone tries to be the quarterback or if everyone wants to be the kicker. Some people won't be fast enough, skilled enough, or strong enough for a certain position. Although they have determined their life's purpose, they won't be able to achieve their true potential until they are training for the position that they are meant to, or called to, play.

Although I loved football, it wasn't my meal ticket. In fact, I never made it past the first year of Division 3 football. Even though I had to accept that football wasn't going to be my way to provide for my family, my commitment to myself, which ultimately drove my calling, wouldn't let me give up because football didn't work out. I knew that I couldn't quit just because the circumstances changed. I found another avenue in education, and that became my way to push the generations forward, rather than football.

On your path to finding your purpose, it's important to understand that the place you thought you found your purpose and didn't could end up leading you to your real and true purpose. On the path to discovering your purpose, you have to be open to more than one way because who you are now will completely change when you actually discover the purpose for your life. Again, my purpose was clear: to provide for my family. I had seen my dad not provide, and I realized that it was up to me. But as I pushed past football and into education, I found my position, or calling—education.

What your calling can do for your life, to me, is nothing short of astonishing. When it is found, it changes your entire perspective on life. You see, I didn't think I was quite smart enough to graduate from college. In fact, the last thing on my mind at eight years old was doing well academically. I didn't enjoy education growing up, or, shall I say, I didn't enjoy standardized education. Like any child, I liked to learn, just not in the way school taught us. So, at eight years old, if you would have told me that education would be my way out instead of football, I would never have believed it.

On your path to discovering your calling, you discover things about yourself that you would have never envisioned. At eight years old, I certainly didn't believe I was smart, but now that I have discovered my "why," you can't tell me I am not. In 2014, I was the first person in my family to have ever graduated from college with a degree, and in 2020, I became the first person in my family to ever graduate with a master's degree.

Being a first-generation college student wasn't easy, to say the least. There were a multitude of challenges that came with it. There is so much you don't know that it psychologically messes with you; the sheer information overload is too much for even the most seasoned academics. The amount of confusion I felt during the first semester left me feeling dumb, stupid, hopeless, and just plain naive. Financially, I didn't even know how much debt I was putting myself into, nor did my parents at the time. I was avoidant about it, and I struggled to pay for school from semester to semester. I had to work on campus at the mailroom, work off campus at a childcare center, and pick up a third job refereeing for youth basketball games. I say all of that to say this: the path to discovering my purpose was hard, and I wanted to give up not just sometimes, but all the time.

But I didn't quit. I persevered with all the resilience I'd built throughout my childhood because I had discovered my "why," my purpose to push the generations forward. My children will never have to experience what I experienced as a child. My children can never say they were a first-generation college student. My children will not go to a campus not fully understanding what they will encounter, and, most importantly, my children will understand the financial implications before they even set foot on any campus. I had to endure it all so that my children will never have to, and that's my purpose.

Pushing the Generations Forward was never about me, even at eight years old. It has always been about helping the folks I care most about and the children that will come behind me. If I make life just a little bit better for the next generation, then I have successfully pushed it forward.

I used to think that pushing generations forward required something huge—a major, life-changing event that would alter the course of history for people like me. I felt like I had to have a million dollars, big houses, fancy cars, and all the stuff associated with the mega rich.

But on the path to finding my purpose, I discovered that pushing a generation forward can be as simple as surviving so that the next generation can thrive. My mother was never able to give us a million dollars, but what she gave us allowed me to never go hungry, allowed us to never be homeless, allowed me focus on what I wanted to do in life, and allowed me to meet one of the greatest men I know: my step-father. He showed up and taught me how to be a man and provided me with the opportunity to become a first-generation college student. My mother survived it all just so that I could do whatever I set my eyes on. She pushed the generations forward.

Whichever way you choose to contribute to the next generation, you have to always ask yourself: "Am I contributing, hurting, or helping?" Even if you have a limited capacity to enact change, you should always choose to help the next generation. If we all had the mindset to help the next generation to come after us, what kind of world would we live in now? No matter what your circumstances are, you have the ability to push a generation forward.

Finding Your Calling

When it comes down to it, your calling will be a unique and specific job designed just for you. Using the football analogy again, your calling will often be determined by your natural size, ability, or strength. Defensive backs and receivers tend to be faster than the other players, and quarterbacks tend to be tall and natural decision makers. Their natural abilities lend themselves to the positions that they play.

The same translates to our life calling. I have always wanted to help people. That was in part because of my upbringing. Because I had an absent dad, I had to find other father figures in my life. That showed me the need for strong leadership felt by others as well. My decision to create and share the Pushing the Generations Forward idea has never been about money; it has always been about this internal desire to give back.

As you are going through the path of self-discovery and looking for your calling, don't ask questions like "How much money will I make? What will people think of me? Is this cool or what people expect of me?" Instead, you need to look for the answers to the following questions: "What will give me a sense of happiness and fulfillment? How can I give back to others?" These questions will guide you to your calling.

Chapter 6

Healing Before Pushing

The body possesses an astonishing and persistent ability to heal itself. Healing comes naturally to the body. In fact, every second we are alive, the cells in our bodies are working tirelessly to bring our body back to balance and harmony. This is known as "homeostasis" or "equilibrium." What it means is that, upon injury, the cells in our bodies spend every minute to heal us back to the normal state. (The Editors of Encyclopaedia Britannica , n.d.)

Although physical healing is natural to the body, this is not the type of healing I want to talk about in this chapter. What I want to talk about is emotional and mental healing. This is the skill to take proper rule over the painful thoughts, feelings, and emotions that occur over the course of your lifetime.

Full disclosure: I am not a licensed behavioral therapist, nor do I want this book to be a substitute for any individual that needs to seek a mental health professional.

My Personal Healing

I struggled for years to heal from the effect of having an absentee father. Not having my father was very tough for me. Growing up, he was never present. He battled with addiction and other things that always kept him away from the home.

Despite that, we still looked forward to the rare days when he was a part of our lives.

One day, my brother and I walked excitedly to the park with our father and our basketball. When we arrived, my dad told us to play and that he would catch up to us after taking care of some business. We nodded our heads and started shooting on the basket.

After a few minutes, we turned to see if our dad was done. He was gone. In fact, he would end up not coming back. What had started out as excitement quickly turned into fear and anger. *How could our dad simply leave us like that? What was more important than us?* Those questions lingered in my head for the rest of my life.

Eventually, my grandmother came to the park and found us, but the hurt was still there. That was the cycle of my childhood: my dad constantly failing to meet even our most basic expectations.

Now, if someone was to ask me, "Kwamane, what is the hardest aspect of adopting the mentality of Pushing the Generations Forward?" I would answer "healing" every time, in a heartbeat. Most Americans will have experienced at least one traumatic event by the age of sixteen. I would argue that the number of traumatic events is higher for youth of color due to systematic oppression, racial injustices, plain ole racism, and so many other systematic factors. Healing can be hard for anyone and everyone.

But the main point I want to get across in this chapter is that although the healing journey is hard, it is absolutely necessary. This is probably where—in the entire concept of Pushing the Generations Forward—you have to think about you. That's because if you do not heal from what has happened to you or what you did in the past, you will pass on those same traumas and mistakes to the next generation.

You may not pass on the exact experience, but you could pass on the coping mechanisms used to deal with what the past has taught. If you do not heal from who or what has hurt you, you could pass down toxic coping skills that will not contribute to a healthy relationship. If you do not heal from past mistakes, you could pass down to the next generation a life of living without self-love or worthiness. It is so easy to unknowingly pass down some of the same toxic traits you are trying to avoid, and if you do not heal, or at least learn to become consciously aware of your emotional limitations, you will only minimally push the generations forward.

Be Honest With Yourself

There are two healing components that I firmly believe will contribute to your efforts in pushing the generations forward. The first concept is accepting that you need to have a real conversation with yourself. It's often hard to do so because of the uncomfortable feelings it may bring to the surface, but it's necessary. The only way you can understand the truth about who you are, why you are, and how you are, is in understanding the whole truth about you—the light and the shadow.

Sometimes, the truth about you might not be easy to accept once you discover what your truth is. You know where you have been wronged, and you know where you have done some wrong. You know when you have been given excuses, and you know the excuses you have given. You know when an opportunity wasn't offered to you, and you know when you didn't take the opportunity offered to you. You know when someone hurt you, but you also know when you hurt someone. When you are having the tough conversation with yourself, you have to make an assessment about which decisions that were made have contributed to where you are in life, and the hard pill to swallow is that some of those decisions were made by you, so there is nobody else to blame.

Let's dive deeper into the decisions which affect your life. Some decisions about your life were controlled by you, some by outside factors, and some reside in the gray area. As stated previously, there are some decisions made by you that did not turn out like you'd expected, and you must accept that. You were in complete control over those decisions and exercised full autonomy, good or bad, and you have to deal with the negative or positive consequences. There are some decisions that were out of your control, and you still have to deal with the consequences of those outside decisions, whether negative or positive. There were some positive decisions made that were good for you, even though it was outside of your control. However, the negative decision making that is outside of your control, but which directly affects you, can be very hard to navigate around and often leaves you feeling hopeless, ashamed, and powerless. We cannot control every event or outcome in life, and that means we cannot control things that are done to us by an individual, a group of people, or even by society. In fact, we can't even change the negative decisions made by us that have already occurred in the past.

However, there is the one thing that we can change, and it's the gray areas. The gray areas are the things we should focus on moving forward with. The gray areas are the things that we do have some sort of control over. What are some of things in life that you do have control over? Your future; your children's future. I am not saying to forget about the past. Instead of focusing on what you did or what someone else did to you, you should focus on the gray area which directly reflects what you are going to do about it.

In society, the gray area doesn't always sound as appeasing as just plain old black and white, and that's okay. I think we can all agree that life isn't black and white, and the gray area is a safe area to pivot and make meaningful changes. If life was black and white, it would be really difficult to make changes, and despite how much life can feel that way, it simply is not. Healing is about understanding what you did, understanding what happened to you, and about what is going to happen to you. You don't get that perspective until you have a real tough conversation with yourself. We can all sit and make excuses as to why, but that would be thinking in black and white. We can all sit around and blame others—and sometimes they are to blame—but the truth is that there are still the gray areas that we have to look forward to.

Forgiveness

The second healing component that contributes to Pushing the Generations Forward is that of Forgiveness. I use a capital "F" here because it is all-encompassing.

Forgiveness feels easy in some cases, but in other cases, Forgiveness feels like an unattainable level in the game of life. To truly forgive someone means to completely pardon them of the offense they committed against you without holding active resentment toward them.

For those situations where it hasn't been easy to forgive, you and I both know that it remains a must. It is a must because if you are not careful while trying to push generations forward, you will mistakenly pass down bitterness and brokenness without even being consciously aware of it.

That's the tough thing about the concept of Pushing the Generations Forward: you have to be really careful what you pass down because if you don't have the discernment to know what's good and what's bad, you could very well hurt the generation you are trying to help. Remember, holding onto resentment is like swallowing poison yourself while hoping your enemy will die.

Depending upon the degree of hurt, you will find it hard to forgive, but you have to because Forgiveness isn't for the person that hurt you; forgiving them is for you. True Forgiveness can lead you down a path of clarity. It gives you a feeling of understanding, empathy, and compassion for the person who did you wrong.

Now, when you hear the word "forgive," it doesn't mean that you have to forget what they did to you, but it allows you to remove the stumbling block they put onto your journey through life. That stumbling block, if not removed, will make it harder for you to push the generation forward, and if you are not careful, your stumbling blocks in life can very well become your children's stumbling blocks.

Now, you cannot speak about Forgiveness without talking about Forgiveness for yourself. Yes, you! You have to apologize and forgive yourself for letting you down. There are some things you did, and decisions you made that were no one's fault but your own. There are some situations that you ended up in life that were solely your own decision. And as Eric Thomas says, "You gotta take the punch that belongs to you." (Thomas, 2015) This means you have to take responsibility for your own mistakes. I am sure they were rooted in past traumas, but they are still your own. If you don't own them, how else can you learn from them? As they say, the first step to recovery is acceptance. Once you have owned your mistakes, then you have to forgive yourself for allowing yourself to make them.

The hardest person to forgive is probably yourself, especially after those moments of self-reflection, but you have to forgive yourself. Once you have forgiven others and have forgiven yourself, you can then fully operate in the gray area which presents itself as an opportunity to push the generations forward and to not focus on what did happen, but what will happen.

Chapter 7

The Mind is the Battleground

As you explore your own potential and how you might push the generations forward, you are likely to come up against obstacles. Many do.

The struggle of many people is facing a sense of emptiness and or nobody-ness in their everyday life. Waking up feeling worthless and depressed, going to bed feeling like tomorrow will just be today but slightly worse—these are the symptoms of a battle in our minds. Your mind can be a battlefield. You might not be an expert of many things, but you are the expert of you. Because you are the expert of you, you have to be able to decipher the truth about you and the lies that you are telling yourself about you. The lies that break into your thoughts and the intrusive contemplations that creep in late at night and stay all day, all week, and eventually, your whole life are things that you can identify and deal with individually, like small skirmishes in the much larger war that you are facing.

Your emotions indicate your true feelings most often. The responsibility that you have is to know your mind well enough that you can trust the thoughts and feelings that act on your values, not just your current emotional state. If you aren't careful, you can allow your current emotions to build a false narrative about you or your life that may not be true.

Yes, you can tell yourself a lie based on how you feel. I can remember in a lot of sitcoms back in the 90s, there was always an episode where you had the main character and a competing mindset, usually played by an alter ego of the main character, representing the battle between good and evil. In most sitcoms, the bad influences usually win the first battle. Why is that? How does that relate about real life? If we are being honest, we have all probably had moments like those ones in the sitcoms.

However, there are always two things that come out of that type of scene. The first thing is that most of the things that were said by the bad side were 100 percent not true. It was all lies and often based upon some false narrative based on how the main character felt in that current moment. Although the shows always had some type of happy ending where the main character was able to get it "right," in reality, we have these moments, and oftentimes, siding with the bad side can be detrimental to your life. Reacting based on how you feel in the current moment can hurt your path to pushing the generations forward.

The next thing that I learned from those sitcoms was that if there is one thing in life you can count on, it is that the truth will always win out. Truth always finds its way to defeat evil in the sitcoms, and this holds true in reality. Why do you think some of the most influential quotes always goes back to the topic of speaking the truth?

> *"I believe that unarmed truth and unconditional love will have the final word in reality. This is why right, temporarily defeated, is stronger than evil triumphant."* – **Dr Martin Luther King**

It is imperative that you start believing the truth about yourself. In this life, you are going to have to argue the truth with yourself, and you have to ensure that you know the truth about yourself in order to defeat the lies you often feed yourself.

I don't know you. I don't know the kind of person you are, I don't know your motivations, and I don't know your mistakes. But, since you are reading this book, I can probably guess a few truths about you; 1) You care about your life—if you didn't, then you wouldn't still be reading this book; and 2) You care about the generations that come after you, and that probably means you care about others. Sure, you may not be perfect, but that's because purpose and pushing the generations forward is never a perfect journey. You have to believe that you have many good traits, and that in spite of what you are feeling in the moment, the negative core beliefs or negative feelings are not the truth.

The truth produces "good fruit," which means the truth produces love, the truth produces awareness, the truth produces enlightenment, the truth produces positivity, the truth produces joy, the truth produces clarity, the truth produces friendship, and the truth produces healthy relationships. Remember the truth, and it shall set you free.

There are a lot of tell-tale signs if you're not telling yourself the truth. Have you ever been hurt badly by something someone said or did, and yet, when asked if you were okay, you responded, "Yes, I'm okay," or "Yes, I am fine," even though you knew deep down inside you weren't? That's because you were subconsciously telling yourself a lie. You know the truth about you, and the truth is you were hurt. The only way to heal from that hurt is to properly process it to include acknowledgement of that and then correct the action. How powerful is it to be able to say to yourself "Hey, Self, you are lying to me right now, and I won't believe the lie for one second!" and then be able to confirm the truth. There isn't one true way of telling yourself the truth; to me, it's a constant battle of the mind.

The battle of the mind can be a dangerous place, and one of my favorite ways to articulate the mind's battleground comes from the Bible: "For the weapons of our warfare are not carnal but mighty in God for pulling down strongholds" (2 Cor. 10:4).

In the Bible, it is recognized that we all will struggle with battles of the of the mind. The battle of the mind deciphers between the truth and lies, the battle for the mind deciphers between good and evil, the battle for the mind deciphers between light and darkness, and the battle for the mind deciphers my feelings and emotions from actual reality. The mind is the battleground, and if you want to push the generations forward, you have to win the mind battle. You have to decipher between the truth and the lie. The truth is you are meant to push the generations forward. The truth is that through you, lives will be changed no matter what your past brought to you. The truth is that pushing the generations will start with you but end with your family line succeeding and thriving and living a purposeful life because of you.

Ways to Win the War

The mind is a reflection of what you feed it. I find it interesting that we have had a major increase in violent crimes, but we don't address some of the most common problems.

We have an increase in the amount of violence that we are feeding are minds on a daily basis. Video games, music, and movies are full of violence, and we consume it daily. The same is true for other issues that are holding us back.

We have a problem spending our money on expensive things that put us in debt, but, again, we are programming ourselves to do it through what we watch. Music videos, rappers, popstars, celebrities, movies, country singers, athletes, and Hollywood tell us that we need these fancy things, and, no matter what we think, we listen because it is so inundated to our culture.

That's why we must win the war by changing what we put into our mind. We will always see these things in our culture, but we don't have to make it our entertainment choice. We can control that.

Instead of catching the next Marvel flick or whatever it is, watch a documentary or course on finances. Instead of listening to the latest country or hip-hop album that is going to drive subliminal messages about sex, money, and drugs to your mind, listen to a podcast that helps grow your mind. The battle can only be won by starting to put the right thoughts and messages in your head through what you consume. Your mind is a product of what you feed it.

Chapter 8

To the Men

Men, I believe that there is an area in society that we have yet to fully address. That area is called masculinity. I bet when you heard the word "masculinity," you immediately thought about the word that always comes with it: toxic. It's time we addressed that conundrum.

Toxic masculinity is real. In my short time of living, I've often been confused by the term, but once you seek first to understand as opposed to being understood, you understand that anything that is toxic does have negative consequences. You see it every day and in so many different mediums that it is often easy to just reject the idea. Toxic masculinity refers to the notion that some people's idea of "manliness" perpetuates domination, homophobia, and aggression.

To put this in simpler terms, toxic masculinity is all about toughness, rejecting anything feminine, power, and control. In most ways, I agree with the definition around toxic masculinity, and agree that these characteristics that define the word are toxic and just plain wrong. There is no way that you can deny the effect that culture has on any person's being. To think that we are different from everyone else in our culture is to deny the way our culture has shaped us as individuals. Nurture has unfortunately made something terrible from what nature intended. We may not want to believe that it is in fact real and affecting us the way that it does. The irony is that as men, this characteristic of invalidating uncomfortable truths is also in and of itself a component of toxic masculinity.

I grew up thinking that being a man, I had to be tough both physically and emotionally. To a certain degree, that's okay, but never to a point where I must bottle up my emotions so that I appear tough just to be called a man. I was born a man, and that alone should qualify me. There were many instances where I was left confused by this idea of "be a man," "toughen up," or "big boys don't cry."

You see, I had to learn how to dry up tears at an early age, and that constant "toughen up" or "be a man" hurt me for a long time emotionally. I still deal with the ramifications of that to this very day.

Burying your emotions should never be an acceptable act for anyone. When you bury your emotions, you only hide them in places where they eventually hurt others. Feelings are like pressure from boiling water. The steam needs to escape and to find a way to go where it needs to go. Nature demands it escape the enclosed environment that it's contained in. If you take that steam and you don't allow it to escape, but instead keep it buried and contained in some airtight container, we all know what happens next: you're going to have an explosion on your hands.

I am a living example and a testament to the fact that your buried feelings are usually influenced by your life decisions. Neither my mother nor stepfather ever enforced the idea of what we call toxic masculinity today. It was something I learned from social media, peers, coaches, and other societal norms.

I recall a truly important time I was left confused by this idea of toxic masculinity. When I was a freshman in high school—what seems like a lifetime ago—I was the second-string quarterback for our varsity football team as a freshman. During the game, I was the next man up. Ahead of me was a senior, and I was the obvious replacement for the starting job next year. It was our last practice of the season, and by tradition, it was Senior Hit Day.

Senior Hit Day is a day where any senior can pick anyone on the team to do the famous Oklahoma drill with. Normally, the seniors see it as a freshman test, and so, they usually pick freshmen as their partners for the drill. I do not remember most of the hits I took, but I remember being called on at least five times by various seniors consistently.

Now, in the game of football, these activities are necessary to a certain extent, and I knew that. After the third time being called, I started to feel a little bit dizzy, but I knew I couldn't show that I was hurt. The fourth time felt like a blur, and in my head, I wanted to say so, but I decided to do the drill.

By the fifth time I was called, I was angry and asking myself what I did to them to make all of the older boys pick me. I was also particularly angry because of the person that called me. He was a six-foot-four, three-hundred-and-fifty-pound offensive lineman. It wasn't the size of the lineman that made me upset; it was the fact that this lineman hadn't played a single snap in a game during the season, and as the second-string quarterback, I probably played in more games than him throughout his entire high school career. Needless to say, he was much bigger than me, and I thought I was more valuable to the future of the team than to someone who barely played.

Before the fifth time, I was a tad bit dazed and confused, and I didn't know it then, but I am pretty sure I suffered a concussion during either the first, second, third, or fourth incident. The big lineman called my name, and I felt irritated and fearful at the same time. I knew that I wasn't okay, but I also knew that I didn't want any of my teammates to think that I was weak or not tough enough. Well, I ultimately selected to do the Oklahoma drill one more time, and I was so glad it was over after that. He got the best of me, and everyone had their laugh. When it was over, it was only in the past and wouldn't affect me anymore.

Although I couldn't remember the details of the hits I took, I remembered how I felt afterward. I was confused, I was upset, and it goes without saying that I was injured. I was confused that even though I stood there and took each hit the way someone tough would do, I didn't feel tough. I didn't feel like I was strong at that moment. I felt weak, and I felt sad. It was because I knew I was hurt, but I didn't have enough guts to say it to my coaches. Despite having every right to say no, I didn't say anything and just kept taking the hits. I didn't stand up for myself and chose the approval of others over my own self. Toxic masculinity was prioritized over my own safety and health. I could have seriously injured myself, but I wanted to be tough, and I wanted others to think I was. This was my experience with the phrase, "man up." My stepfather came into my life and taught me how to stand up for myself, and I know if he had been there that day, he would have certainly not have been happy with that decision I made that day. In fact, he would have put an end to it himself if he thought I was hurt in any way. Before him, this was how men were supposed to act, in my mind. The understanding that I had at the time was that incidents like these were just part of living and there was no alternative.

Men, if we want to push the generations forward, we have to normalize being able to articulate when we are not at our best or when we are hurt or weak, and we have to accept that those phrases like "man up," "be a man," or "be a big boy" should be considered toxic and goes against the true nature of masculinity. Emotions are not only healthy for men, but they're our right as human beings, and we need to teach our young men this fact at an earlier age. We cannot allow the next generation to go through life thinking they have to sacrifice their mental, physical, and emotional health to appease societal constructs.

There is such a thing as healthy masculinity. Not all versions of the masculine man are toxic. Imagine a world where masculinity was associated with healthy communication and honest expressions of vulnerability and emotions. What if we lived in a world where men expressed emotions and expressed the need to be validated? Let's be honest, menfolk, we like being validated. As humans, we naturally crave it. It's how we form our identities—and there is nothing to be ashamed of. We like our actions to be noticed and appreciated the same as any other gender, but the difference is we have a problem saying it. What if we lived in a world where men acknowledged when they felt vulnerable and felt that it was okay to seek out professional or personal help? What if the new "man up" was an encouragement to open up honestly and to be vulnerable?

Acknowledging that you are feeling vulnerable should be a sign for men to get help either from loved ones or professionally because, oftentimes, when we feel vulnerable as men, we feel the need to get tougher or go to our mental burial ground to pretend that we can bury deep and forget about it.

Nothing hidden stays that way forever. My mother would always say that what's in the dark will always come into the light, and that's the same for this scenario. No matter how much you try and bury your vulnerabilities, they will always rise to the surface where they need sunlight.

What if we lived in a world where we, as men, treat women and other races and sexualities with equality and respect? Gender roles play a huge part in a balanced and harmonious system, and if any part of that system becomes flawed or broken, it throws the entire system off, and so, there is a need for each individual role. What this looks like in terms of a relationship is when a man is the "man of the household" who is making his partner feel inferior.

The purpose of gender roles is to keep everyone responsible for their own tasks and to keep relationships working for the people involved. But, when we make it the role of a man to hide his feelings, to lie about how he feels, or to dominate and oppress his spouse, his family, and his children, then we are throwing a system into disunity and throwing the balance off in an otherwise balanced and fair system. Your role is not one of superiority, and your proper role is no harder or easier than that of the other. Balance means just that: evenly weighted on both sides; roles complementing other roles for the purpose of success and harmony. This can only come from openness and respect. Both are hard to gain in their truest and healthiest form in this world. But, working together to help each other achieve this will result in more and more people attaining balance.

No matter who you are or what you believe in, everyone should be treated with respect, regardless of their race, ethnicity, gender, or sexual identity. What if we lived in a world where we respected and valued women? In 2022, why is there a wage gap between women and men? I would argue that it's all rooted in toxic masculinity. Is that something that we want to teach our daughters? That they are intrinsically worth less than men? I would not think so. There is no future in this kind of future. To borrow another quote from the late Malcolm X, "If you're in a country that reflects the consciousness toward the importance of education, it's because the woman is aware of the importance of education."

A future is only as good as the men and women that drive it forward. Historically, it was only as good as the women involved in that movement and the effect that they have on the society at large. Women can adopt the mentality to push the generations forward in a lot of the same ways men can. It is not only restricted to giving birth, as many have said in the past. The worth of a woman is more than her biological capacity to conceive. The struggle of the women in our society who push the generations forward is that they face different stereotypes and tropes.

One person's burden may not be colored, shaped, or fit the same way, but if it bears down on them heavily and causes their knees to grow weak, then it is a burden nonetheless. We cannot be distracted by the shape of the struggle. The worth of any person is inherent. It's intrinsic. In the same way, so is their ability to create change and to drive movements and societies forward. The ability to push the generations forward is something that can be found in the heart of anyone, no matter their gender, age, or how they identify.

The truth is, men, we can live in a world where we can be vulnerable. We can live in a world where we express feelings and the need to be validated. We can live in a world where we treat everyone—and I mean everyone—with respect and equality. We can live in a world where we value women. We should be passing this type of world to the next generation.

A safer and kinder world, one where men can be open and honest, is possible. But it requires us to make sacrifices. Maybe we'll be scorned and maybe even called some things that we don't like to be called today. Maybe we'll think that it's just going to end with us and that all we're getting out of it is just the rebuke and the disapproval for our actions. Men, if we tackle toxic masculinity correctly, the next generation won't have to fight for justice and equality. The next generation of men won't have to suffer mentally. The next generation won't have to live in sadness because they feel there is something wrong with them based on someone else's skewed beliefs. That's why we have to push the generations forward to make this world a better place.

Chapter 9

The Missing Father

The subject of the missing father, this story that is told so often by people who have grown up with sadness, confusion, and in many cases, anger, is one that creates so much conversation in popular culture that it's impossible to ignore. Now, you might say this chapter could have easily gone with the previous chapter, but I feel the conversation is important enough to be written about alone. It's one of the great divisions for many people who are looking to break generational curses.

The absent father takes with him the love that he could teach to the son or daughter. From there, the child grows up and has to figure out how to communicate things that they were never taught. They have to discover an entire identity on their own without the lessons that someone in their life was supposed to teach them. There's little difference if that father died or simply left. The feeling of being lost and not knowing where to find the answers is still there. The days that could have been spent learning or growing are turned into days that the child then has fill on their own. For those who pick this book up, the feelings of anger against an absent parent may be fresh or may be long gone. But, either way, there is a time to sit and consider the effects that this has had on the individual and on the family that individual will raise.

I was at the park one day with my niece. While watching her play at the playground with some of her friends, I noticed a young boy and his dad playing basketball. The reason it caught my attention was because

I kept hearing the dad say, "Aww, almost! Try again!" repeatedly to his son, who was trying to complete a basketball activity in which the objective was to do a simple under-the-leg cross over with a spring to the basket lay-up. The young boy could easily make the lay-up, but he missed the basket the majority of the time. He was far more effective in completing the second half of the activity than the first half of the activity.

The young boy, over and over again, attempted the under-the-leg crossover, and with each attempt, he was not successful. In fact, with most of those unsuccessful attempts, he ended up falling to the ground or tripping over his own feet. The young boy was becoming extremely frustrated, and all I kept hearing from the father was "Aww, almost! Try again!"

After several more failed attempts, the young boy became incredibly frustrated and yelled, "I can't do this the stupid crossover!" He kicked the ball and ran off the court to sit on the sideline.

I became extremely intrigued by what the dad was going to do next. His dad went over and picked up the ball and calmly walked toward his son. By this time, I was so interested in what the father was going to say to the son that I walked closer to the basketball court just to hear it.

The father asked the young boy, "Are you okay? What's wrong?"

The son explained how he was feeling, and tears started to roll down his face. "I can't do the stupid under the leg crossover."

Before the son finished, the dad wiped the tears from the boy's eyes and said, "Aww, almost … Try again?"

The young boy stated, "No, I can't do it."

The dad said to the little boy, "Son, you can do it, you just have to keep trying. I wasn't good at it either, but do you know what I did? I kept working and working until I was able to do it, and I know you can do it if you try again. Believe in yourself, and I know it's hard, but I know you can do it."

Moments later, the young boy got up, walked toward the court, and, still listening to his father who was coaching him in the background, lined up for the activity one last time. He said to himself, "I got this," and went for the cross over. While certainly not perfect, he did the under-the-leg cross over and went for the lay-up and, to my surprise, made the shot.

The young boy was overjoyed as he ran to his dad with a hyperactive "Let's goooo!" and gave him a high five.

As the dad was congratulating and praising him, I heard his voice crackle, and he began to wipe tears from his eyes. I didn't even know the young boy, and I felt happy for him.

When my niece and I drove home from the park that day, I had a chance to process what I had just witnessed. I had witnessed a teachable moment between a father and a son.

After pondering it a little more, my happiness was short-lived. I immediately began to think about the little boys or little girls who are on the playground, or in the classrooms, or at home who will never hear "Aww, almost! Try again."

You see, in the moment, it sounds like just a phrase, but in life, it becomes a mantra of hope and a constant voice that can never be taken away. The "Aww, almost! Try again!" speaks to grit and resilience, confidence and empowerment. I became sad for other little boys and girls who will never experience a moment of coaching from their fathers. I felt sad for the little boys and girls who will never know that whatever they are feeling, someone else has felt it too. I pictured a little boy on the sideline with his head down because he quit and had no one there to help him by saying, "Aww, almost! Try again."

The help of a loving father is something that many young people have not been able to experience. It's one of the areas of life that you can make the largest impact in by being there, as a parent, and realizing that your impact on the world starts at home. "Believe in yourself, and I know it's hard, but I know that you can do it," is a phrase that any young man waits to hear and desires so strongly to be motivated by. The feeling of love, acceptance, and support in those words are things that many do not feel. It's moments like this, such pivotal and significant moments, that are there to help drive people in the direction that they should go. Without any such support, the future of that little life that could be achieving great things can be greatly changed and possibly even turned the wrong direction permanently.

I spent most of my early childhood without a father, and as I talked about earlier, my father quit his life for drugs and alcohol. I remember those moments when I needed him and he wasn't there. I needed someone to teach me about my first elementary crush. I needed someone to teach me about my first bully. I needed someone to teach me about confidence. I needed someone to teach me about integrity and responsibility. I needed someone to teach me about emotions. I needed someone to teach me about resilience. I needed someone to teach me adversity. I needed someone to coach me through the mental blocks and hardships life threw my way at an early age. The things I needed aren't things you discover magically one day; they are things that should be coached and taught from the early and formative stage of childhood all the way into adulthood. In life, there is no substitute for the coaching that a father can give.

Luckily, my stepfather came into my life, and he was able to fill in the gaps, but I feel for the little boys and girls who will never hear that voice of their father in those crucial, teachable moments. They will never know the comfort that I felt. For them, the struggle is filling those portions of their hearts where the comfort of a father should have been.

Whatever your dynamic with your father was—maybe, like me, you lost your father to substances, or maybe your father passed away before you could hear his voice, or maybe, for some reason, you have never met your father—I am here to let you know that I feel you and understand what you have or are going through, but despite those circumstances, you still have to push the generations forward.

You cannot change what happened to you, nor can you change who wasn't there. You can ensure that your children will never have to experience what you experienced with a missing parent. Breaking the generational cycle requires you to be there and to be present for them when they need you.

In some ways, I saw myself in the boy on the sideline of the basketball court that day. Just like the father in that moment, I vowed to be there for my children when they needed me to say, "Aww, almost! Try again."

Maybe as a father, you have missed out on those moments, and you feel bad about it. The good thing about pushing the generations forward is that it's never too late to start. Pushing the generations forward will never be a perfect process, but it is an everyday mindset to try and get it right. Be there for your children, to support them and to encourage them, and be there for the next "Aww, almost! Try again."

Chapter 10

The Closing

As we come to the final chapters of this book, I hope I have inspired you to start a new chapter in your life. Yes, there were probably things that I could've addressed in more depth. Maybe I could've elaborated and impressed by sharing more of my knowledge, but that was not my goal. I wrote this book to give you the steps to guide you into a new way of life, a new mindset, a new driver for your selected purpose—a life or mindset where our future generations can live empowered, successful lives. While I don't know what you are going through or why you even picked up this book, what I do know for certain is this: You owe it to yourself to push the generations forward. You owe it to all who will come after you to push the generations forward.

The actions that we have to take may be difficult to maintain over time. It may require intense willpower to develop the proper mindset. It may even take your whole life to train yourself to maintain it and live it as your reality. Nothing good comes overnight, and everything good requires patience.

All people of all ages have important lessons to pass down from their unique experiences. I have to be honest with you though: this process of generational empowerment will not be easy. It has never, not for the entirety of the human experience, been an easy task to push major changes in a society. You are going up against the generational trauma that has been developed over generations and generations—it can be found in your genetic code.

Understand this: These generational challenges didn't start with you. It started with your ancestors. As Black & Indigenous People of Color, you understand first-hand what generational trauma looks like. It's not pretty, nor is it easy to overcome. The complete genocide of indigenous people under colonial rule is still linked to present day social, economic, cultural, and political inequalities. The slavery of millions of Africans who were bought here in chains and the Jim Crow laws and the civil rights era—the effects of these are still present. From the millions of Asian Americans who were forced into brutal internment camps, to the millions of Hispanic Americans who were barred entry into White establishments and were forced to live in impoverished areas with limited resources and education, it's still seen everywhere, effecting life down to the everyday.

Pushing the generations forward can seem almost impossible. You not only have to deal with the present, but you have to constantly be reminded of the past, and the past can hurt. The past can hurt so much that you feel hopeless and lack the motivation to make the changes needed in your life. As I look down my family tree, I see folks who were affected by these terrible circumstances, and my grandparents had it way harder than I ever would. Although we know racism and oppression still exist, it was more normalized and prevalent back when my grandmothers were still alive, but, somehow, they survived. In times like today, when it is still so difficult, there is hope everywhere, much more than was available to them at that time. Even though life might feel hopeless, it's important to know that you still need to push the generations forward. If your ancestors were able to survive lynching, hangings, seeing their children being sold, racial killings, mass murders, forced imprisonment, and constant rape, then you too can survive your situation—because your ancestors survived; they pushed it forward. It's your job and your duty to take it to the next level.

By no means am I saying you have to forget about your own hardship or not speak up against oppression both generally and systematically, but you cannot let those things be the reason why you quit. You cannot let the pain and hurt be the reason why you give up on your family. You cannot let your mistakes be the reason why you give up. Nothing can be allowed to make you quit. Your place is here, and your time is now. Let all of those things—the hardship, mistakes, oppression, racism, and hurt—be the reason why you must definitely push the generations forward. If you don't, where will your children, or their children, end up? Will they end up being a product of the same old environment, or will you change their lives for the better?

The choice is ultimately up to you. The answer to those questions lies in the actions that you take and the words that you say. It's not just a question to be pondered but actions that need to be taken. So, rise up and move. Get your feet on the right path and train your mind and your body. Teach yourself daily what you need to do and how you need to be. If you also follow through in your mindset and your healing, if you apply yourself to these principles and don't simply forget the things that you've learned here, then you can move mountains and bring change.

From here, we have to spread the word. Tell everyone you know and live it through your language as well as through your actions. Don't just hide these secrets and let them die with you. Instead, live up to the goals you've set for yourself for all to see. There's this idea that success works in silence. And that may be true for when you're building a dream for yourself and need to avoid being braggadocious or need to avoid negativity from others. But this is not how movements begin. They begin with one voice speaking to another voice, and that voice then speaks to another voice. The spread of information, the dissemination and diaspora of knowledge is where movements sprout and spread, like seeds on the wings of birds or on the breeze. You are the wind that will carry them to every soft patch of soil near you and plant that truth in their hearts. Then you too will drive movements and will push the generations forward.

But I wouldn't stop there. Strangely enough, I would turn to the Almighty, and say, 'If you allow me to live just a few years in the second half of the twentieth century, I will be happy.' Now that's a strange statement to make because the world is all messed up. The nation is sick. Trouble is in the land. Confusion all around. That's a strange statement. But I know, somehow, that only when it is dark enough can you see the stars. And I see God working in this period of the twentieth century in a way that men, in some strange way, are responding — something is happening in our world. The masses of people are rising up. And wherever they are assembled today, whether they are in Johannesburg, South Africa; Nairobi, Kenya; Accra, Ghana; New York City; Atlanta, Georgia; Jackson, Mississippi; or Memphis, Tennessee — the cry is always the same — 'We want to be free.' – **Dr Martin Luther King**.

Chapter 11

Be A Mover

Everything that I talked out in this book has the ability to change your life. Learning to navigate your thoughts, restructure your mind, and find your purpose will truly make you more able to transform your life and the lives of those around you.

I believe that the first step in pushing generations forward is to have access to the right knowledge and resources. While there is much more to be said on the subject, I believe that the topics I covered are enough to set you on the path to self-discovery and will lead you to make a positive change.

However, I do recognize that no amount of knowledge can replace action. We have found ourselves in the situations and circumstances we are in today because of the actions that our ancestors have taken. Some of these have been good, and some of these have been bad. Either way, we are here and have a responsibility to take the next action—the next step. Because of this responsibility, I want to leave you with this last story—a challenge and an encouragement combined.

The Servants and Their Talents

There is an old biblical parable about a master and his three servants. A rich master leaves his magnificent mansion to go on a luxurious vacation. Upon his departure, he tells three of his closest servants, "I am entrusting each of you to a portion of my money, invest it for when I return."

Several months later, he returns. Two of his servants returned his money with the profits they had made while he was gone. He was very pleased and rewarded them for their efforts. The third servant returned his master the money he had given him without any additional profit.

Seeing the disappointment of his master, he said, "I know you are a hard master, and I didn't want to mess up and lose your money, so I buried it." In other words, he said, "I let fear keep me from taking action."

The master was very upset. He took back the money, stripped him of his responsibilities, and gave them to the other two servants who had taken action.

(Biblica, 1984)

Every human being is faced with this same opportunity. We have been given a gift to use and must choose to bury it or pursue it. The lesson is clear; it doesn't matter what knowledge you have and how much you learn, you must take action. The greatest shame would be for you take what you learned in this book and do nothing with it.

Movers and Non-Movers

In reality, we are all the same as these three servants. Every human is given the same three gifts: time, energy, and intellect. We are given these gifts with the expectation that we will use them. One day we will lose these gifts. Some of us take these gifts and use them to improve our lives and the lives of those around us, bringing a return on the gift they were given. These people are called "movers."

The most obvious movers are inventors, entrepreneurs, or world changers. George Washington Carver was a mover. He had the same gifts of time, energy, and intellect that others had before him. However, he was not content to be ordinary. He had to move. Because of him, we have multiple ways to use the peanut in food, agriculture, and other industries. He improved our farming methods to allow for healthier crops and more sustainable farming methods. These inventions and discoveries changed the world and allowed him to build a fortune for his family as well.

The important thing to notice is that not all movers have extreme financial wealth. Martin Luther King Jr. is an example of a world-changing mover. He was given the same gifts as every other human being before him. He, however, led a movement that changed the rights of many Americans. Rather than accept the way the world was, he created a movement. He used his time, energy, and intellect to champion for the rights of a people that were denied many basic American freedoms.

Other movers to consider would be Malcolm X, George Washington, and others. What each of these men had in common was the ability to move in a way that changed the way the world moved. They could not simply follow the path of those that had gone before them. They sacrificed the comfort of staying still and risked their livelihood to *move* and *change* the world.

Movers are people that we look up to because of their ability to affect change on the world around them. They tend to have several common traits, which include:

- A sense of higher purpose
- Insatiable curiosity
- Hyperness
- Deep thinking
- Solution-minded
- Tendency to lead
- A strong desire to create
- Charisma
- Action taking

"Non-movers" are people that bury their gift of time, energy, and intellect. They settle for being average, and they constantly make excuses and talk about what could have been. Just like the third servant, they end up living disappointing lives and do not accomplish much of anything. They stay set in the same course for the entirety of their lives.

A non-mover has two common traits: ignorance and fear. A large portion of our society has been turned into non-movers because of a lack of knowledge and understanding. Ignorance blinds people to reality. A non-mover thinks that a mover is inherently different. A non-mover thinks a mover must be unique or have a special talent, and that is why he or she is able to accomplish great things.

The truth is we all have the ability to be movers. We all have the same three gifts of time, energy, and intellect. The only difference is whether you use the gifts and take action or bury them in the ground.

The second trait of a non-mover is fear. In my opinion, this is worse than ignorance. A fearful non-mover has realized that he has the ability to move but fears the unknown. He is fearful of others' opinions and inadequacy, or fearful of sacrificing the comfort of the norm to be a mover. Before you start picturing people that you know and labeling them as non-movers, realize this important truth: we are all non-movers until we learn to take action.

Common Traits of Non-Movers:

- Wishful thinking
- Constant complaining
- Endless excuses
- Fear of the unknown
- Problem-oriented
- Tendency to follow
- Lack of creativity
- Lack of focus
- Never take action

Final Challenge:

So, as you are putting this book down and looking to go on with your life, I want to ask you this simple question: Which one are you?

Are you a non-mover? Will you take this information with you and continue living as you have? Or will you be a mover? Will you take this knowledge and turn it into something more?

It is easy to find ourselves gushing in the stories of powerful people from our past, especially if they had a direct effect on your culture and history. This is good, but we must realize *we have the same ability to affect a change around us. We simply have to take action.* I hope this book was an encouragement to you. I hope it was educational, but, more importantly, I hope it spurred you to take action.

My final question is this: *Will you be a mover? Will you take the action necessary to push the generations forward?*

Bibliography

Biblica. (1984). *The Holy Bible (New International Version)* . Biblica, Zondervan, and Hodder & Stoughton .

BrainFacts/Sfn. (2012). Neuron Conversations: How Brain Cells Communicate . *BrainFacts.org*, 1.

Carol S Dweck, P. (2007). Mindset, The New Psychology Of Success . In P. Carol S. Dweck, *Mindset, The New Psychology of Success* (p. 320). Ballantine Books.

King, D. M. (1967). MLK Talks "New Phase of Civil RIghts Struggle, 11 Months Before His Assassination . (S. Vanocur, Interviewer)

Kotlawī, A. Y. (n.d.). *Akhlāq-uṣ-Ṣāliḥīn.* Karachi, Pakistan: Maktaba-tul-Madīnaĥ.

Mindset Works . (n.d.). *The Science* . Retrieved from Mindset Works: https://www.mindsetworks.com/science/

The Editors of Encyclopaedia Britannica . (n.d.). *Britannica Homeostasis*. Retrieved from Britannica: https://www.britannica.com/science/homeostasis

Thomas, E. (Director). (2015). *YOU OWE YOU* [Motion Picture].

CPSIA information can be obtained
at www.ICGtesting.com
Printed in the USA
BVHW090304200822
645019BV00018BA/736